"... A tiny bug cannot comprehend the entirety of the universe cohesively and completely, as it hasn't got the capacity. We have the capacity but our purpose and point of focus does not include understanding the entirety of the whole of existence precisely while our point of focus and materialization or manifestation exists in the third dimension. Understanding that we are not the limited, unimpressive mere egoic humans pursuing our desires to our detriment or betterment may yet buoy humanity as they work their way through the construct of this experience here in this world, in this dimension at this time."

~ Rev. J.L. Harter

The Ego is the Veil

OTHER BOOKS BY AUTHOR:

Poetry Series:

Ravenous Reflections
Spiritual Reflections
Ethereal Reflections
Love's Eternal Reflections

Spiritual Growth and Understanding:

Changing Perspectives: The Journey is the Destination
Expanding Horizons: Growth and Beyond

The Life Series:
Life – The Journey Continues
Life – The Journey Continues - II
Life – The Journey Continues – III
Life – The Journey Continues – IV
Life – The Journey Continues – IV

Spiritual Fiction (Conceptual Exploration):

The Chronicles of Aliyah

Ministry of Connected Consciousness:

The Impact of Reincarnation on Health and Well-being
The Ego is the Veil
Solving for X (Coming Soon)
So It's Over. Now What?

The Ego is the Veil

///

Rev. J.L. Harter

Published by

The Ministry of Connected Consciousness
Fountain Valley, CA

Printed in the United States of America.

Cover photo: J.L Harter

First Edition

ISBN: 978-1-312-30889-3

Acknowledgments

"The Ego is a veil between humans and God" is a partial quote by the 13th Century Sufi Mystic poet, Rumi. I wish to express my deepest gratitude for this great poet and spiritual mystic for it is his works and words and those of the same or similar spiritual path and thought process that inspired me to pursue ever greater understanding of the need for the merging of thoughts from multiple disciplines such as those from Philosophy, Metaphysics, Physics, Spirituality, and Psychology to work with others in greater harmony. These applied science and other disciplines serve as valuable keys to facilitating the improvement of the human condition as I see it. So too do I wish to express my sincere gratitude to the human race incarnate and those beings present but not incarnate, for helping me through every day living and being perfect just as they are and thereby helping me to understand this quote, what it means, and why it has become such an interest for me personally.

I would also like to specifically acknowledge my partner, Dr. Liam Leonard who encouraged me to pursue the field of study of most interest to me (Metaphysics and Psychology), helped me to understand the framework of study and research and who has been with me in discussion of the concepts of my dissertation along with being my favorite editor. I am sincerely grateful for his friendship, patience, understanding, love, and support.

Table of Contents

Preface

What if the "veil" isn't out there somewhere but rather inside of us right here in the form of our ego? I wonder. We talk of many things as if they are "out there;" outside of ourselves and as we learn and live this life, understanding begins to dawn and we come to realize that as above, so below...as within, so without. During times of meditation or selfless service, the veil seems to thin for us and we feel bliss or true love. When we thin the veil of the ego, we begin to feel the truth from the core of our being without the ego arguing for pole position in this situation or that situation.

I think the veil; the thing that separates us all is the ego. The ego or veil, has a perfectly good purpose. I don't think either was supposed to be destroyed or in anyway eradicated. Instead, the ego and the veil it seemingly creates should be understood. We can thin the veil thereby minimizing our egos by setting our intent, turning our ego-self over to the greater Soul-Self thereby piercing the veil and all sorts of amazing things are then possible. Things we could never have imagined from within a thick veil of the ego can then be created positively. Consider, if we over-identify too much with the ego in an unhealthy way, (and oh goodness are there oh so many unhealthy ways), the veil is thick around us and we are cut off from not only Source but each other as well. The conclusion I come to is that the thicker the ego or veil, the greater the perceived disconnection from Source and others. This can unwittingly occur due to unnatural beliefs or other unhealthy means of existence and can be a very challenging way to learn in this life.

So, I come to understand that all is truly perfect as it is whether or not I judge it densely veiled within my own ego or not. Even the ego and the veil are perfect. They are perfect for each soul's journey regardless of the dimension of the ego or veil. All things in good time come through the thinning of the veil or ego, like love, compassion and understanding. I wish to explore this "thinning veil" concept a bit more. I didn't come up with this idea entirely on my own. It was a little nugget of a puzzle I was left with as I considered the nature of my own ego and the veil and a trusted guide from somewhere seemingly not here and yet right here left me to ponder...and ponder I did.

This work began as my doctoral dissertation during my course of study with the University of Sedona. I researched a number of texts and realized that many other well-versed spiritual teachers and pioneers in new age thought were pointing to the same conclusion I was coming to. Within this work, I explore the concept further, again with the intent of bringing greater understanding to our existence and how we may use this information to experience a better life.

As I mentioned in my last publication, *The Impact of Reincarnation on Health and Well-being*, I intend to research the various concepts of consciousness and hopefully find greater understanding to share with those who are interested. This work is the second in a series with the third to follow as a deeper exploration into consciousness. I hope you'll enjoy the journey of this exploration into consciousness.

With love and great blessings,

J. L. Harter

Chapter I – Introduction

I selected for book, the topic of the ego and the "veil" in spiritual terms and its impact on the facilitation of spiritual growth and understanding. I chose this topic, as it is one I am more than familiar with. It is the understanding of this topic that made me realize its key value in undertaking the facilitation of guidance for those interested in spiritual growth and achieving a greater sense of well-being.

In my long-standing observation, the problem that I'm seeking to explore and address within this work is that without clearly understanding the correlation between the ego and veil and their true purpose, it is difficult, if not impossible to help bring about true understanding of the pathways to spiritual growth and healthier living. The concept of the ego is considered to be well understood in the discipline of Psychology. The concept of the veil has been contemplated for ages by those engaged in spiritual or religious study. But I think that more focus should be brought to the light in terms of greater understanding that the ego and the veil are one and the same and better yet, why that may be a good realization from which we begin to work.

As with my last work, I will make use of the review of additional literature on the topic of consciousness, ego and veil. My literature review will cover the concepts of the ego and the veil both. These seemingly unrelated topics coalesce neatly into a concept within which can help interested individuals to understand their lives, the actions, and resulting outcomes that either brings about pleasure or pain. Through this understanding healing methods can be employed to help individuals reach deeper within and allow the true depths of transformation to come forth giving them greater tools with which to employ for the gain of greater positive strides in life and well, more successful living. Without deep understanding of how these two concepts collide in reality, in the etheric realms even, we are limited in our approaches to guiding those interested to their own light. It is this concept to me that is of primary import if we are to be of true and honest assistance to humanity while questing to finding greater meaning in life.

My literature review will cover various texts that will include, but not necessarily be limited to, the fields of Psychology, New Age thought, and Spirituality as well as Metaphysics. There are those rare and precious individuals in this world who innately understand the connection between ego and veil as well as physical and non-physical reality who know they work in union to our ultimate betterment. I will explore the works of these individuals and I assert that our challenge in helping individuals find greater fulfillment in life is due to the lack of more informed tools and clearer understanding of origins, the source, true source of the challenges set before us.

As I craft this work, I am most interested in expressing the importance of what is right before us and within our reach physically, mentally, and spiritually to help us achieve that which we are most interested in achieving. I wish to outline that through greater knowledge and understanding of some key concepts, we can reach farther with our efforts to move into a new era of understanding all of the resources available that stem from this concept I have selected for exploration. I move to the focus of this concept through the explorations and documentation of those well and little known individuals who understood completely or understood without necessarily having full comprehension by virtue of their words and works that began to point to the truth.

These educated teachers and authors outline the impacts they have had not only on their respective disciplines but many individuals throughout the world with their research, their writing, their distilled understanding of complex concepts and they began to paint a picture. The picture they painted respectively, collectively added to an emerging body of knowledge and that knowledge is that we are by far more than just simple biological beings. Yes our hearts beat and blood pumps through our veins, we live, we love, we contribute to society in some way either physically or energetically but we are still more. We are conscious beings with free will. We have aspects to our consciousness that are very complex. Our consciousness is stratified in more ways than we have fully studied but many fields are doing more and more work to gain greater understanding. If we begin to take a look at where these learned individuals began and continue to build upon their findings with an open mind and in the true spirit of collaboration for the greater good of all of humanity, who knows what we could accomplish?

I feel very strongly that it's important to understand the information that is out there whether or not it is readily available as definitively proven. From this, we then begin to understand the information in practical terms and how it may help with practical application by more who may be interested in this topic. Through that broader understanding, assisting human beings achieve greater health and a sense of well-being is truly paramount to making this world a better place, in my own opinion.

Within this work, I'm going to explore two basic themes through the filters of multiple disciplines and alternative fields of study. I'm going to research literature from the fields of Psychology, the Theosophy Movement, Physics (light), Spirituality, Metaphysics, and New Age thought. The first theme relates to the ego and the consciousness that defines and stratifies it as we understand it more commonly today. The second theme is an exploration of the concept of the veil as has been used in countless religious, spiritual, mystical, and New Age texts and practices.

This study will utilize a single methodology via a literature review. From the works I have selected for their thematic impact on my topical focus, I will explore the two concepts, how they intersect and support my contention that these two separately seeming concepts are one as well as the need for further study in potentially even new disciplines or preferably, across multiple disciplines working in harmony without prejudice for greater support and understanding for the sake of humanity.

I will outline my personal explorations of the literature on both the ego from the perspective of consciousness and the veil and outline how it is this understanding and the further explorations thereof that are needed in order to provide ever greater tools, resources, and assistance to those seeking to improve their lives and help themselves and their loved ones thrive in ways they never imagined possible. My own personal experience in these concepts have been long-standing and it is also this expertise that has helped facilitate my work as a spiritual counselor, providing guidance to those seeking greater health and happiness through an improved sense of positive health and well-being. Understanding these concepts also helped me to exist in this world with an ever increasing sense of harmony.

The Ego is the Veil

Chapter 2 – Research of Existing Works

Within this section, I will begin with the review of the more traditional academic disciplines, as this is necessary to add to the fullness of understanding. I will move from there into spiritual disciplines that also carry these themes from alternative perspectives. For my literature review I have selected some well-known groundbreaking thinkers in the world of Psychology, Theosophy, Metaphysics, Physics, Spirituality and New Age thought. These authors, perhaps without realizing it, touched on the same themes using different perspectives filtered through the eyes of their respective disciplines and created an exciting place to start my explorations. The concept of consciousness is key to our well-being. These authors and teachers contributed a great deal to facilitating a better life for so many in their respective ways through the exploration of consciousness; the ego and veil.

The Ego and the Id

The Ego and the Id is a brief work of Dr. Sigmund Freud. In this work, Dr. Freud outlines the psychological concepts of consciousness. Dr. Freud discusses that consciousness exists essentially at three levels. The first level is consciousness as awareness itself and the other two are varying levels of unconsciousness. Dr. Freud defines the three levels consciousness thusly:

1.   Being Conscious – A descriptive term, resting on perception of the most immediate and certain character;

2.   Latent Consciousness – which is unconscious but has the capacity to, at some point, rise to the point of awareness in the conscious mind; and

3.   Repressed Consciousness – which is not able to rise to the point of direct awareness in the conscious mind (Freud, n.p.).

Dr. Freud abbreviates these terms for ease of reference:

- Cs. (Conscious)
- Pcs. (Pre-Conscious–Latent)
- Ucs. (Unconscious–Repressed)

(Freud, n.p.)

Dr. Freud outlines the ego as the first point of contact with the outside world. More specifically, the ego is a part of the Id modified by the effects of the outside world. Freud goes on to explain another process of interacting consciousness as a complication between the ego and Id. He refers to this as the "ego-ideal" or "Super ego." Within this work, Freud begins his descent into defining the underpinnings of psychoanalysis *vis a vis* the formations and growth or lack thereof, of the various levels of consciousness. Because the underpinnings of psychoanalysis and sexual ideations teaming therefrom (as primarily founded by Dr. Freud) laced throughout the remaining portion of this text is not the point of focus for my dissertation, I will stop at these most pertinent concepts from this source. My focus in this book is the concepts of consciousness of which, Dr. Freud clearly understood and outlined. This understanding has been used by the psychological discipline to facilitate study, form various therapies, and to assist in greater understanding and growth of the field of Psychology.

The Undiscovered Self

Within this book that contains one of Dr. Carl Jung's essays that focuses on consciousness from a self point-of-view and outlines or summarizes some of the passionate points of the focus of his work. Dr. Jung outlines in point after point in this brief writing that man cannot truly understand himself because man is more than just a physical body, mind, and consciousness. The conscious aspect of man is seemingly known in what he is aware of and is unfortunately obfuscated by parts of his own unconsciousness—the unconscious aspect of the psyche.

Dr. Carl Jung describes that "states" (as a collective) and "religions" (another form of collective) engender and promote a mass consciousness that circumvents individuality as well as physically and psychically enslaves man through the psychic attack of fear and hate. In the opinion of Dr. Jung, both state and religion foists itself as God-like or the saving grace of man. The psyche knows better but unless man becomes aware of his own lack of awareness, he fails to become free; he submits to the veil and those who would ensure its place is solidly maintained as a barrier.

A direct quote from Dr. Jung in this work expresses the focus well:

> Separation from his instinctual nature inevitably plunges civilized man into the conflict between consciousness and unconsciousness, spirit and nature,

knowledge and faith, a split that becomes pathological the moment his consciousness is no longer able to reject or suppress his instinctual side. (79)

Another quote from Dr. Carl Jung's work represents the importance of the unconscious:

> For more than fifty years we have known, or could have known, that there is an unconscious as a counterbalance to consciousness. Medical psychology has furnished all the necessary empirical and experimental proofs of this. There is an unconscious psychic reality, which demonstrably influences consciousness and its contents. All this is known, but no practical conclusions have been drawn from it. We still go on thinking and acting as before, as if we were simplex and not duplex. Accordingly, we imagine ourselves to be innocuous, reasonable and humane. We do not think of distrusting our motives or of asking ourselves how the inner man feels about the things we do in the outside world. But actually it is frivolous, superficial and unreasonable of us, as well as psychically unhygienic, to overlook the reaction and standpoint of the unconscious. (81)

Dr. Jung seemed to truly understand the shortcomings of the superficial approach to Psychology and consciousness. His interest in the unconscious, the soul and spirit of humanity as well as his dreams seemingly uncontrolled is evidenced in his reach a fair bit broader than most of his contemporaries. The remainder of this particular work dealt with the challenges of his political time in the world and provided some moral food for thought. While Dr. Jung seemed a bit conflicted in terms of religious experiences he clearly felt the importance of self-awareness through the unconscious was paramount to creating positive change in the world.

The Undiscovered Self with Symbols and The Interpretation of Dreams

The *Undiscovered Self with Symbols and The Interpretation of Dreams* is a book that outlines the work of Dr. Carl Jung in the form of a collection of his essays. The first part of this book was published in another book I have selected for my literature review so I won't repeat that portion. For this review, I shall focus on the second essay in the book. The second essay was actually excerpted from Volume 18 of the "Collective Works of C.J. Jung, The Symbolic Life," (1955 by Princeton University Press). In a portion of the book that focused on his essay, "Symbols and the Interpretation of Dreams," Dr. Carl Jung takes you through the path of greater understanding of the psyche, of consciousness, attention of the ego, and the inattention of the subconscious. Dr. Jung focuses on the signs and symbolism both in life in the conscious state and that of the unconscious state in the world of dreams. Dr. Jung discusses the reality of symbols, their multitudinous meanings to the perceiver, and even categorizes some of the symbology into archetypal perceptions.

He further elucidates the reader on the reasons that humans, as they have become ever more civilized, has stepped further away from nature and what is natural and stepped further into intellectual creations. Through the resulting sense of the loss of meaning, humanity compensates through the symbolism manifested in their dreams as our conscious attention reigns ever more supreme, the unconscious, or other side of the veil, will continue to reach our awareness grasping our attention through our dreams and the subliminal triggers of unconscious experience.

Discovering Psychology

Discovering Psychology is a textbook commonly used in collegiate introductory Psychology courses across the U.S. This textbook provides a broad overview of all aspects of Psychology from its humble beginnings as a discipline springing from Philosophy to its common understanding today. It covers Psychology's roots to psychological research and typical diagnostic processes. Again, my focus is not specific to the study of Psychology in and of itself but of an aspect of it that is germane to the focus of my dissertation. Dr. William James is written about in this book as one of the fathers of the discipline of Psychology. In one of his quotes included within this textbook, he touches on my point of focus, "Even though your conscious experience is constantly changing, you don't experience your personal consciousness as disjointed. Rather, the subjective experience of consciousness has a sense of continuity." (*Discovering Psychology*, 135)

The concept alluded to in this particular quote led Dr. James to research and consider consciousness as a "stream" or "river." From the text is another specific quote from Dr. James:

> Consciousness, then, does not appear to itself chopped up in bits...It is nothing jointed; it flows. A "river" or a "stream" are metaphors by which it is most naturally described. In talking of it hereafter, let us call it the stream of thought, or consciousness of subjective life (*Discovering Psychology*, 135).

Within this book the authors outlined the key contributors to the field of Psychology from its humble beginnings to its present-day use in terms of understanding human behavior, the various forms of therapy and likely causes as well as effects of mental illness. Because the majority of this book was not the focus of my review, I've not included the entirety of the detail. I wished to focus on consciousness from the early days of Psychology as a discipline as it forms the basis of the concept of ego.

The Secret Doctrine – Abridged and Annotated

This book abridges, annotates, and explains the concepts written in Madame H.P. Blavatsky's great esoteric work, *The Secret Doctrine*, (1888, unknown). Within her original work referenced in this book, H.P. Blavatsky sought to summarize and explain the teachings she received on the cosmogony of the universe from various teachers she encountered in the East. While my focus is not on the topic of Theosophy or esotericism specifically, there are aspects of this work relevant to my focus of metaphysical psychology or the ego is the veil as Mme. Blavatsky sought to explain the origins of the entirety of the universe. She is quoted in Michael Gome's work in one particular section as follows:

> The Lipika Circumscribe – The Triangle, the first one (The vertical line or the Figure I), the cube, the second one, and the pentacle within the egg (circle). It is the ring called "pass not" for those who descend and ascend (as also for those) who, during the kalpa, are progressing toward the great day "Be with

us"...Thus were formed the Arupa and the Rupa (the formless world and the world of forms); from one light seven lights; from each of the seven, seven times seven lights, the "Wheels" watch the ring. (40)

Within the following paragraph after this stanza, the author describes the esoteric meaning of the stanza is that:

> . . . the Recorders of the Karmic ledger, make an impassable barrier between the personal EGO and the impersonal Self, the Noumenon and Parent Source of the former. Hence the allegory. They circumscribe the manifested world of matter within the RING 'Pass-Not.' (40)

Although this is a much older work than the two previously referenced, it is clear to me in its reading that there is consideration and perhaps deference given to it being a fact that the ego and the veil serve the same purpose. That purpose would be to prevent those descending into Earth consciousness from ascending to the beyond worldly existence via the ego/veil until such time as each soul is intended to pass beyond the veil. Another quote from this work I would like to include here due to its relevance, "On account of the Essence of Aether, or the unseen space, being held divine as the supposed veil of Diety, it was regarded as the medium between this life and the next one." (140)

16

Interestingly, this book describes the congruence between various documented descriptions of cosmogony in line with modern Physics, Metaphysics, Theosophy, and Theology. The ability of The Secret Doctrine to elucidate and unite multiple disciplines and thought processes, even if through the use of abstract language is fascinating. It also consistently defines the ego and veil from ancient understanding that still today exists if even often at a superficial level. The wisdom of the ages is contained in summary and as other works before and since, continues a common theme apparent throughout most works of religious, philosophical or metaphysical nature.

A Seth Reader

This book is a collection of some of the most popular works put forth by Jane Roberts who channeled the entity Seth. Seth, as formerly channeled by Ms. Roberts, claimed to be a multi-dimensional entity or over-soul and through several channeling sessions through the medium, her husband Rob Butts, documented Seth's advice, explanations, historical tales, philosophic, and spiritual advice on a wide range of spiritual, psychological, and metaphysical topics. There are numerous sections within this book that address specific advice and focus of the channeling sessions. The topics covered were vast and ranged from simple ego and consciousness to religion, God, and reincarnation. However, my focus in utilizing this book in my literature review is more along the lines of the process of channeling.

In the Introduction to this work, edited by Richard Roberts, Richard provides an explanation of the history of spiritualism, which includes channeling. An important focus of the process of channeling has been excerpted from Richard's explanation below and is include here as it relates to my realm of the exploration of the ego and veil:

> For the most part, the mediums, or 'channels' as we call them today, operated within the framework of a small 'church' an ordinary hall or parlor frequented by regular members all known to one another. Donations were accepted on a collection plate passed during the 'service.' Shamanistic trance, a valid religious tradition for hundreds of centuries before, became the means whereby the medium's spirit guides came through. In terms of modern psychology, we can think of this as a simple transfer of consciousness from left-brain hemispheres to right-brain. Although the medium may appear to be unconscious, he or she is indeed speaking intelligibly. Thanks to Jung and the infant science of psychology, we have learned that the unconscious mind 'knows' more than the

conscious mind, that is, the length and breadth of its knowledge transcends the factual world of the senses. Now when the medium enters trance, the spirit guide, or controlling consciousness comes through. Spirit guides run through spectrums ranging from the omniscient to the divinely ludicrous. Indeed, one may generally regard the exalted state of the guide as an attempt by the medium to exalt his or her own status with the public, making that particular person suspect, in my eyes at least. (5)

The description and history of channeling and experiences noted by Richard Roberts, who indicates he is a psychic investigator, help provide a bridge of understanding into the world of channeling. Another excellent quote, also from the introduction refers again to one of my favorite doctors of Psychology, Carl Jung. Richard states, with regard to why some channelers seek to defraud the public:

> The answer lies, I think, with C.G. Jung's revelations about the personal unconscious and its links to that treasure-trove of archetypes, the collective unconscious . . . However, the unconscious is conscious, and not just in our dream life. We know our animus or anima through our psychological projections onto others of Mr. or Miss Right, our ideal man and woman, for surely if we have fallen in love we have projected the qualities of our own animus or anima onto

the object of our love. Most of all, these archetypes desire communication with the conscious mind, and frequently in the case of women manifest as a voice, which if the animus is negatively constituted, makes critical comments upon her character and conduct. If the animus is positively constituted, he may speak as a disembodied higher consciousness, seemingly from "outside" herself, presenting her with higher teaching . . . . (6).

Within this book, Seth reveals the nature of reality, existence, personal consciousness, and purpose of the framework within which we create what we wish to experience. In another amazing quote from this work, this time from Seth:

There is nothing wrong with the concept of an egotistically based individual being: I am not suggesting, therefore, that your individuality is something to be lost, thrown aside or superseded. Nor am I saying that it is should be buried, submerged or dissolved in a superself. I am not suggesting that its edges be blurred by a powerful unconscious. I am saying that the individual self must become consciously aware of far more reality; that it must allow its recognition of identity to expand so that it includes previously unconscious knowledge. (162)

Seth's line of thinking seems to corroborate my

own thought that the ego is something to be understood and not eradicated. He also ties in the concept that ego, consciousness and unconsciousness are a part of our reality. In this work, certain themes emerge such as the thought that consciousness is not separate from an individual or the entirety of the universe.

A Course in Miracles

A Course in Miracles is a channeled work as given through Dr. Helen Schucman and who with her associate Dr. William Thetford, brought forth several volumes of channeled instruction from Jesus into a modern day methodical approach to viewing life in a way that frees one's self from the many illusions of this place or life on Earth. After reviewing the Course and actually working through its lessons and descriptions, it is not hard to arrive at the conclusion that the premise of this work in part is that the ego is the veil. The Course speaks of forgiveness as the passageway to freedom from the illusions of this place. If viewed through a purely spiritual perspective you can see its design is to detach the control of the strictly egotistical view of this world thus freeing the students of the Course from the illusions of it. Through understanding and forgiveness, one can become free and return to a state of harmony.

The Ego is the Veil

There is a wonderful quote from the Course taken from the introductory section, "Knowledge is a truth under one law, the Law of love or God" (x). This text is a Course in understanding the nature of our existence, our perceptions, cause, effect, and the need for understanding. The premise on which the concepts of this book stand are that we are one with God, that at a core level we have taken on guilt due to our separation through consciousness, and that although we perceive separation, it is unreal. All that we perceive is unreal and when we learn forgiveness we set ourselves free and return to love.

When one steps back from this work, one can intuit the connection between ego and consciousness and that ego is the illusory veil that seemingly disconnects us from our Source. In another direct quote, *A Course in Miracles* illustrates this concept:

> The Ego is the questioning aspect of the post-separation self, which was made rather that created. It is capable of asking questions but not of perceiving meaningful answers because these would involve knowledge and cannot be perceived. (42)

The Course seeks to free individuals from the illusion of duality through teaching them to right their thinking through exercises daily. Another quote that helps illustrate my point of focus is,

"Consciousness, the level of perception, was the first split introduced into the mind after separation, making the mind a perceiver rather than a creator. Consciousness is correctly defined as the domain of the ego . . ." (42).

The Tao of Physics

The Tao of Physics compares and contrasts the scientific discipline of Physics with the alternative discipline of Metaphysics and spiritual practice. One of the quotes from Fritjof Capra within this work outlines a portion of my focus:

> When the rational mind is silenced, the intuitive mode produces an extraordinary awareness; the environment is experienced in a direct way without the filter of conceptual thinking. In the words of Chang Tzu, 'The still mind of the sage is a mirror of Heaven and Earth – the glass of all things.' The experience of oneness with the surrounding environment is the main characteristic of the meditative state. It is a state of consciousness where every form of fragmentation has ceased, fading away into undifferentiated unity. (39)

The author has collected numerous quotes from learned doctors of physics and psychology as well as Hindu, Tao, Zen, Buddhist and other spiritual and metaphysical disciplines. He depicts in this work, the similarity of the experiences versus scientific study and the limited nature of language to accurately articulate the full scope and detail of their findings. All are really explorations of the same Source from varied angles and practices. I included this particular resource, as it is also evidence of the ego and the veil, in my opinion. This includes making progress through discovery by finding ways to get beyond it (ego) to the truth of a thing or object (peering through the veil).

To support my focus from another perspective, I need to draw on the world of Quantum Physics as is outlined by Fritjof Capra in the following quoted text:

> The following discussion is based on the so-called Copenhagen interpretation of quantum theory which was developed by Bohr and Heisenberg in the late 1920s and is still the most widely accepted model. In my discussion I shall follow the presentation given by Henry Stapp of the University of California which concentrates on certain aspects of the theory and on a certain type of experimental situation that is frequently encountered in subatomic physics. . . Stapp's presentation shows most clearly how quantum theory implies an essential inter-connectedness of nature, and it also puts the theory in a framework that can be readily extended to the relativistic models of

subatomic particles to be discussed later on. The starting point of the Copenhagen interpretation is the division of the physical world into an observed system ('object') and an observing system. The observed system can be an atom, a subatomic particle, an atomic process, etc. The observing system consists of the experimental apparatus and will include one or several human observers. A serious difficulty now arises from the fact that the two systems are treated in different ways. The observing system is described in the terms of classical physics, but these terms cannot be used consistently for the description of the observed 'object'. We know that classical concepts are inadequate at the atomic level, yet we have to use them to describe our experiments and to state the results. There is no way we can escape this paradox. The technical language of classical physics is just a refinement of our everyday language and it is the only language we have to communicate our experimental results. (132)

The author describes part of the challenge of the experiential perspective of the ego in part herein. He sheds light on another important point when he states that, "Quantum theory thus reveals an essential interconnectedness of the universe. It shows that we cannot decompose the world into independently existing smallest units" (137).

The author diverges from the technical scientific aspects of physics and science and paints the similarities in the unity of all things through ancient spiritual texts. A good example illustrating further the points the author intends to make and one I wish to use for my own purposes to be later described comes from Eastern thought:

> The picture of an interconnected cosmic web which emerges from modern atomic physics has been used extensively in the East to convey the mystical experience of nature. For the Hindus, Brahman is the unifying thread in the cosmic web, the ultimate ground of all being: He on whom the sky, the earth, and the atmosphere are woven, and the wind, together with all life-breaths, Him alone know as the one Soul. (139)

The cosmic web is important to my point of focus for it is understanding the cosmic web and its component parts manifest that we begin to better understand why the ego is the veil.

The Power of Now

Through the author's own life challenges and observation of his own thought process he took apart the dismal seeming reality of his existence at a particularly challenging point in his life. Through observation and analysis of his own thoughts, a spiritual teacher was born as if shot through the dark on the tip of the lightning bolt of truth. A direct quote from Mr. Tolle's in *The Power of Now* describes a moment in time when he was quite depressed. He shares the following quote to illustrate the moment he became aware of his consciousness:

> 'I cannot live with myself any longer.' This was the thought that kept repeating itself in my mind. Then suddenly I became aware of what a peculiar thought it was. 'Am I one or Two?' If I cannot live with myself, there must be two of me: The 'I' and the 'self' that 'I' cannot live with. 'Maybe' I thought, 'only one of them is real.' (4)

The author then discusses the peace that came with his understanding that the thinker of the thought was unreal and the observer of the thought was real. It brought him more than just great peace. It brought him greater understanding of the Source of Truth. The author writes:

> Later, people would come up to me and say: 'I want what you have, can you give it to me, or show me how to get it?' And I would say: 'You have it already, you just can't feel it because your mind is making too much noise.' That answer later grew into the book that you are holding in your hands. (6)

The author posits that you already have within

27

you a great peace and connectedness to all that is. He reminds the reader that you cannot "think" your way free of the ego. A direct quote from Eckhart Tolle expresses this well:

> You already understand the mechanics of the conscious state; identification with the mind, which creates a false self, the ego, as a substitute for your true self rooted in being. 'You become as a branch cut off from the vine.' As Jesus puts it. (47)

This author well illustrates the concept of the ego representing the veil between reality and illusion. I do believe based on other works from this author, he's not done illustrating what he has come to understand and what others also are coming to understand and will find better ways to articulate once the words align more aptly with the feelings of truth inside them. *The Power of Now* helps the readers to better understand that the ego's perception is not necessarily the only reality and through understanding this point, an individual can invite the reality of the fullness of their true being into a fully awakened and aware conscious existence. It is this kind of aware conscious existence that may improve the outlook, health and well-being of humanity.

Chapter 3 – Perspectives

The methods I have used to support my arguments were derived in part from a comparative analysis of existing thought from a variety of disciplines. My explorations test my overarching premise, which focuses on *the ego is the veil* against positions held in each of these well known disciplines and perspectives. These learned perspectives encompass Philosophy, Spirituality, Metaphysics, and some aspects of Physics along with elements of Psychology.

This rigorous analysis is achieved by examining the key or relevant themes in existing literature as is outlined in the literature review. It is important to note that the exploration I am presenting requires a methodology that allows for a critical analysis of the various disciplines listed above. Therefore, an integral aspect of the methodology is repeated application of the explorative question within each discipline; this provides the outcomes with its hypothesis and its validity.

The Ego is the Veil

My findings as a result of the review of literature, my own first hand experiences as well as other reading on this topic affirms my own thoughts that the ego is the veil but perhaps language is much too limited to comprehend the fullness of the meaning of these words or the implications they have on the wholeness of our being.

In a way, it seems I'm attempting to define what has seemed impossible to define. The ego is consciousness and the veil is that intangible spiritual religious theme we keep bumping up against in terms of our beliefs. But what if it is just that we lack the proper framework or that we limit ourselves so much by our beliefs that we just won't allow ourselves to theorize new hypotheses fresh by throwing out belief all-together? The ego is consciousness in the physical. The veil, in some ways is that intangible unconsciousness and beyond it, possibly into the All of Everything. How can you properly string words together coherently and cohesively enough to even have such an argument? It isn't easy and while this concept came out of an idea I felt was given to me from beyond the veil, in order to describe what came with that little idea was an entire down-load of meaning in the form of feeling that isn't so easy to articulate. So, I face what very likely, all of the disciplines face when trying to box in the abstract with aspects that are not entirely provable or even fully definable with the applied sciences or other disciplines. Regardless, I feel compelled to try.

In the following chapters, I explore my thoughts and bring in the thoughts of greater minds than mine to touch on the points where we seem to connect in congruence and then step outside of the box a little bit with further explorations and questions.

So, on with the show. I will begin by exploring within subsequent chapters where I've been in reviewing the literature, the observations I've made with each review and what the various disciplines have had to offer as they touched upon this conscious theme that has much greater impact than any of us may have realized.

The Ego is the Veil

Chapter 4 - The Contributions of the Discipline of Psychology

I began my research with Dr. Sigmund Freud, the pioneer of psychoanalysis and another pioneer in the explorations of human consciousness shortly after Psychology became its own discipline. Freud studied the personality and the impact consciousness had upon it. Freud began to see consciousness emerging in distinct stratifications, which became common understanding after a time. From Dr. Freud's perspective, the ego is where consciousness meets the world. Pre-consciousness is the place we store our memories and can serve as a bridge between consciousness and unconsciousness. In the work Discovering Psychology, Dr. Freud is quoted:

> Freud (1904, 1933) believed that the unconscious can also be revealed in unintentional actions, such as accidents, mistakes, instances of forgetting and inadvertent slips of the tongue, which are often referred to as 'Freudian slips.' According to Freud, many seemingly accidental or unintentional actions are not

accidental at all, but are determined by unconscious motives. (*Discovering Psychology*, 421)

Freud, in the discipline of Psychology began to unravel the layers of the fullness of our being but seemed to stop at those first superficial discoveries even if they were not at all insignificant to the field of Psychology. His work gave us a greater understanding of the ego and its next closest relatives in consciousness. Had he kept going and studying I cannot help but wonder if he would have discovered so much more. He started to point in the direction of the veil without seemingly, to understand that he was pointing at anything other than expanding awareness of consciousness. In this quote, from his essay in, *The Ego and the Id*, Dr. Freud conveys the results of his study of consciousness succinctly:

> Being Conscious is in the first place a purely descriptive term of the most immediate and certain character. Experience goes on to show that a physical element (for instance, an idea) is not as a rule conscious for a protracted length of time. On the contrary, a state of consciousness is characteristically very transitory an idea that is conscious now is no longer so a moment later, although it can be again under certain conditions that are easily brought about. (Stellar Books, n.p.)

The significance of this concept helped found his methodology for psychoanalysis which is still used by practitioners today but although profound for its time, times have changed and advances in consciousness from multiple disciplines are shedding ever more light on the wholeness of our being calling for more than just the initial stages of the understanding of consciousness. Dr. Freud contributed a great deal of knowledge on the topic of consciousness and our understanding of the ego. Within my literature review I came across another quote directly from Dr. Freud from *The Ego and the Id* about the ego that illustrates my point, "We have formed an idea that in each individual, there is a coherent organization of mental processes; and we call this...ego" (The Ego and Id, n.p.).

Continuing my research into the discipline of Psychology, a number of well educated doctors of Philosophy, Physiology, Biology and Science began to join the discipline bringing with it even greater understanding of consciousness as I found in researching briefly one of the early founders of Psychology, William James. Dr. James very aptly described consciousness in terms of a stream or flow, which implies active motion and movement. He may or may not have understood the fullness of that which he described but he too began to point in the direction of the ego and the veil. If consciousness is, in fact a stream, where does that stream begin?

I rounded out my research on the ego and consciousness reviewing the works of Dr. Carl G. Jung, a disciple and contemporary of Dr. Sigmund Freud. Dr. Jung built on the work of his contemporary concerning consciousness and moved into a level much deeper, in fact, a more spiritual approach one might conclude. Dr. Jung's work concerning the collective consciousness is well known, his study on archetypes, and the anima and animus again start to point in the direction of a deeper aspect to the unconscious mind than he seemed willing to go publically, at least. Even the lengths he went were considered at the time to be mystical and for the time, it was ground-breaking work that continued the deeper research into consciousness and the psyche. It seemed Dr. Jung knew a great deal more spiritually speaking than he published, likely for reasons of academic stature. In one of his quotes from his essay on the "Undiscovered Self," he states:

> Most people confuse 'self-knowledge' with knowledge of their conscious ego personalities. Anyone who has ego-consciousness at all takes it for granted that he knows himself. But the ego knows only its own contents, not the unconscious and its contents. People measure their self-knowledge by what the average person in their social environment knows of himself,

but not by the real psychic facts, which are for the most part hidden from them. (6)

In this statement it would seem that Dr. Jung implies that the ego is a veil to our true selves. From his perspective: "the ego cannot know itself" and perhaps in that time in history, this made sense. But over-time more study and experience added to the whole body of understanding and new conscious thought emerged that further builds on Dr. Jung's findings. But this new conscious thought emerged in other disciplines beyond psychology, as my further findings will show.

Even Dr. Jung must have contemplated this with a further statement from a second essay series in the book, *The Undiscovered Self with Symbols and the Interpretation of Dreams*, when he stated, "A sign is always less than the thing it points to, and a symbol is always more than we can understand at first sight" (92). Dr. Jung even seems to contemplate the idea further when he stated in the same text:

> In all higher grades of science, imagination and intuition play an increasingly important role over intellect and its capacity for application. Even physics, the most rigorous of all the applied sciences, depends to an astonishing degree on intuition, which works by the way of the unconscious processes and not by logical deductions . . . . (131)

The Ego is the Veil

Chapter 5 - The Contributions of the Theosophy Movement

In the combination of Philosophy, Theology, and spiritualism which became a part of the Theosophical movement in the late 1800's by its founders Madame Helena Blavatsky and Henry Steel Olcott, we find a much more spiritual approach and understanding to consciousness and its greater source and purpose. Within her work, *The Secret Doctrine*, (1888, publisher unknown cited from *The Secret Doctrine* annotated and abridged by Michael Gomes) Madame Blavatsky describes the veil. In the abridged and annotated version of *The Secret Doctrine* by Michael Gomes, he states:

> There can be no manifestation of Consciousness, semi-consciousness or even 'unconscious purposiveness,' except through the vehicle of matter; that is to say, on this our plane, wherein human consciousness in its normal state cannot soar beyond what is known as transcendental metaphysics, it is only through some molecular aggregation or fabric that Spirit wells up in a stream of individual or sub-conscious subjectivity. And

as Matter existing apart from perception is a mere abstraction, both of these aspects of the ABSOLUTE – Cosmic Substance and Cosmic Ideation – are mutually interdependent... From the standpoint of the highest metaphysics, the whole Universe, gods included, is an illusion; but the illusion of him who is in himself an illusion differs on every plane of consciousness; and we have no more right to dogmatize about the possible nature of the perceptive faculties of the Ego on, say, the sixth plane, than we have to identify our perceptions with, or make them a standard for, those of an ant, in its mode of consciousness. (132)

Within this work both the original topic author and the author of this book seem to be directly pointing to the ego or consciousness being the veil between ego consciousness and Cosmic Consciousness. There seems to be implied an understanding that ego in the physical world is conscious, physically awake and yet there is this aspect of existence beyond the veil where consciousness goes but the physical cannot.

Chapter 6 - The Contributions of Spirituality

Within the realm of Spirituality, I turned to *A Course in Miracles* (the Course). Having been a student of the Course for many years, I find many parallels in thought between various disciplines concerning the ego and the veil. In one quote from the Course the authors state:

> The Ego is the questioning aspect of the post-separation self, which was made rather than created. It is capable of asking questions but not of perceiving meaningful answers because these would involve knowledge and cannot be perceived." (42)

The Course posits that the ego is the veil between our God-Conscious selves and our Ego-Conscious selves and is the source of our guilt, shame, and other challenging emotions requiring the forgiveness of sin in others, therefore bringing forgiveness to self for the purpose of liberation from the guilt of separation from God. In another quote from *A Course in Miracles*, "Consciousness, the level of perception, was the first split introduced into

41

the mind after separation, making the mind a perceiver rather than a creator. Consciousness Is correctly defined as the domain of the ego . . ." (42).

Considering that the channeler of the Course material was well versed in Psychology and would have been well studied in the foundations that support it, clearly there is an understanding that the ego is what stands between human beings and the Truth. That Truth being, that we are not ever disconnected from Source and that all we perceive in the world is unreal, is an illusion of a limited perception, and can be forgiven through love thus rejoining an individual to the Divine Source.

The Course begins to more directly point to the ego and veil concept and although I find the work beautifully written and stated with pure intent, I do not find it is the end-all be-all approach to what ails the hearts and minds of humanity. Channeled works are just that. They do not necessarily represent the entirety of the Truth but rather that, which has been perceived through the receiver of the messages (the translator). Even still, the concept of the ego and veil are pointed to in these great works.

Also within the realm of Spirituality, I turned to *A Seth Reader* (Roberts, 1993). The topic of channeling itself, much like the Course mentioned earlier, are to me evidence of one's ability to set aside the ego (veil) and reach right into the world of the unconscious or, rather, the Cosmic or One Consciousness from which all knowledge is available. The channeled topics of Seth as documented by Jane Roberts span a great deal of knowledge that extended beyond that which the channeler held. Whether that was because she was truly reaching beyond the veil or tapping into the collective consciousness (which Dr. Carl Jung was famous for addressing) is unknown and cannot be empirically proven.

However, clearly for channeling to be of true service, the channeler cannot, while in normal egoic consciousness open themselves up without moving the veil of that egoic consciousness to reach beyond it. From that point, information from beyond normal consciousness can be experienced or obtained and shared. Many a religious work was similarly inspired from the *Christian Bible* to numerous Eastern religious texts and more. The New Age and Spiritual sections in bookstores and online are filled with volumes of channeled works. Many of these works speak of meditation and the preparation for it which does involve stilling the mind (ego) and normal waking consciousness and slipping into deeper levels of consciousness and sometimes that state in between to allow one to peer beyond the veil.

The Ego is the Veil

Chapter 7 - The Contribution of Physics and Metaphysics

Through the light exploration of my focus into Physics and the deeper metaphysical aspects of existence conveyed by Fritjof Capra in *The Tao of Physics*, we begin to speak in a slightly different language about what are similar concepts. What is true at the microcosmic level is true of most things at the macrocosmic level (as above, so below). Astrophysicists and Biologists may find synchronicities in their work at the macrocosmic and microcosmic levels. So too can Physics, Metaphysics and Spirituality together come to similar conclusions. One quote in particular from *The Tao of Physics* that illustrates my focus on the ego is the veil is stated as follows: "... When the rational mind is silenced, the intuitive mode produces an extraordinary awareness..." (39).

When the ego is brought to a state of silence, stillness or gently set aside, the other side of the veil can be reached and the observer is then enriched with experiences one might not otherwise experience with the ego's constant labeling, chattering, comparing and contrasting. Another aspect physics brings to the table without a specific spiritual aspect is illustrated in an excerpt from the well known theoretical physicist, Michio Kaku in his book, *The Future of the Mind*:

> The idea of consciousness has intrigued philosophers for centuries, but it has resisted a simple definition, even to this day. The philosopher David Chalmers has cataloged more than twenty thousand papers written on the subject; nowhere in science have so many devoted so much to create so little consensus. (41)

With Dr. Kaku's quote, he points to the fact that there are multiple explorations by various disciplines into the realm of consciousness but yet the data collected is inconclusive in terms of what consciousness truly is.

Physics and Metaphysics may vary from the strictly scientific view to a blend of the potential spiritual view but they seem to both come back to consciousness in some way in their explorations of what it is we are as we contemplate our existence and the vast array of real and potential experiences. It seems there is a large body of thought on ego from a scientific point of view and the veil from a metaphysical point of view and while both sides may not agree on their approaches, they do seem to agree that what we may be dealing with is not entirely known or well understood enough to fully and accurately articulate.

The Ego is the Veil

Chapter 8 - The Contribution of New Age Thought

Eckhart Tolle, in *The Power of Now*, describes an entirely new thought process that touches on the concept of ego and veil but in a different way. The concept of stilling the mind by observing its thoughts in the absence of judgment is another way of setting aside egoic control (or veil) that robs an individual of peace. In early Psychology some of our most famous psychologists are quoted herein indicating that consciousness cannot know itself.

Here Eckhart Tolle challenges this thought process. Consciousness can know its conscious thoughts and therefore know it is conscious. Through the knowledge of the ego-consciousness in motion, one can separate from the egoic thoughts and return to a state of the observer. But what is this observer and why has it not yet been adequately defined by the applied science disciplines? The academic disciplines have provided a model and concept from early in the development of Psychology as a discipline but it seemed to stop short at Spirituality or Metaphysics. Philosophy seems to believe that consciousness cannot be defined at all. Spirituality, Metaphysics, and the new thought that stems from these disciplines of another but no less important kind, seems to build on Psychology and lean more towards a philosophical Spirituality. The ego and its processes are a mere form of superficial consciousness that when focused on without judgment can be quieted, brought to stillness and peace and openness to what lies beyond physical consciousness.

With this author's concept of observing the ego, one can experience this at any time or any place. The noticing of one's thoughts is quite simple and needs no testing to occur other than pointing out to an individual when it is observing itself as consciousness. This was really a breakthrough in New Age thought and as the author indicates repeatedly, all have the ability to observe their own thoughts from the position of observer thus disengaging purposefully from the ego's emotional thoughts and thereby coming to a place of much greater peace.

One of many challenging aspects to the concept of the ego equating to the veil in the way I intend to focus on it is that both concepts may be widely accepted within the confines of their respective disciplines or alternative practices but neither is empirically proven to exist in definitive ways consistently. If we take the term of "ego" by itself and consider it in the terms of consciousness alone, I think layperson and scientist alike would agree that ego has been proven in that we all have conscious aspects of identity or personality. The field of Psychology would tell us that our minds have also been proven to hold conscious and unconscious aspects, with the unconscious aspects existing at only two levels that are physically related as in the case of Dr. Sigmund Freud and his contemporary, Dr. Carl Jung. Dr. Jung went a step further contemplating a collective consciousness, which at the time, bordered on the mystical and is not too unlike the Metaphysical perspective.

Some neurobiological studies would have us believe that the mind is only a function of the brain and its systems within the body system and this is based on the studies that they have conducted with all the rigors required of the applied sciences. However, as is stated in his paper, "Consciousness: Still a Mystery," John Hicks states:

> Given the accepted principle that every moment of consciousness has its neural correlates; the crucial question arises, Which produces which? Most neurophysiologists work on some highly specialized area of brain research and are not particularly interested in the philosophical issue, as they see it, of the relationship between brain and consciousness. For it does not make any practical difference to them whether

consciousness is identical with, or caused by, or only correlated with brain activity. But those who do concern themselves with this fundamental question distinguish between the easy problem and the hard problem. The easy problem—easy in principle—is to trace precisely what is going on in the brain when someone is consciously perceiving, thinking, willing, experiencing some emotion, creating a work of art, etc. The hard problem is to find out what consciousness actually is and how it is caused—assuming, as they mostly do, that it is somehow caused—by cerebral activity. This, says Steven Rose [Director of the Brain and Behavior Research Group at the Open University, UK], is "science's last frontier.

We can't really have a discussion about ego and not isolate for discussion the concept of consciousness. If Psychology and Biology or the specialty areas of Neurobiology within their fields have relegated consciousness to only the realm of the mind dependent upon bodily systems and neurologic synaptic processes of the brain, I think we begin to fall short of what consciousness is in its entirety. Michio Kaku points out some interesting arguments in his book *The Future of the Mind* that indicate the brain is a translator and without it's full faculties functioning properly, translations of normal everyday things and activities cannot be named much less understood. I think science proves this is accurate but it is still only part of the picture. The learned scholars in the applied sciences are right to point these findings out. The problem is I think we start from a premise of disproving possibilities, meaning that we are biased before we begin. When we start to get into consciousness, all bets are off for me as I have experienced consciousness in ways that indicate there is much more to the story than can be empirically proven at this point in time.

Consciousness goes beyond the functions of the brain and body because it existed before the body and will exist after the heart stops beating. There seems to be an aspect of consciousness that still today is merely hypothesized and not yet clearly understood. What we term "consciousness" can seemingly be clearly tested by most with little effort. Ego and its function as defined by Psychology as consciousness, fall within the realm of concepts developed to describe a state of being or focus as awareness.

The veil could, within the confines of these disciplines, be understood as the point at which the opposite of consciousness begins to occur but yet by the psychologically defined term of consciousness and then the related term unconsciousness simultaneously exists within a being at the same time. If we turn to Biology, it is simpler in that consciousness holds more of a meaning of awareness or responsiveness to stimulus through the brain or its neurobiological synaptic activity.

The Ego is the Veil

In the realm of the spirit or Metaphysics there is a concept of Cosmic Consciousness that is relegated to the realms of the soul, spirit or the ever-after concept if one subscribes to that belief system. But belief is far from empirical evidence of anything as belief represents an untested hypothesis. Metaphysics and Spirituality give us some wings to fly with different ideas and experiences whether or not the concepts can be empirically proven. If it were not a mere hypothesis, it would not be a belief but would rather be definitive truth or knowledge.

I have to step back for a moment to the point at which this journey or concept began for me. It began with a concept from an ancient mystic, with the statement that: "The Ego is the Veil that separates man from God," (Rumi, unknown). When you begin to understand ego in psychological terms and consciousness from psychological and spiritual or metaphysical terms, the picture begins to form a little more or at least begs the question, what is it (consciousness) really? If we identify only with the egoic thought, we cannot go beyond the egoic thought. We cannot know our consciousness. As my literature review showed, consciousness can be observed by the conscious soul. This is something expressed by Eckhart Tolle who wrote about his personal experience in observing his own conscious thoughts. In another work along a similar vein, Peter Ralston describes a similar experience with regard to understanding the consciousness of self in his work, *The Book of Not Knowing*:

> Just as suddenly as a bubble bursting, my mind opened up to a new level of consciousness, and I felt my familiar sense of self completely dissolve. It seemed like my awareness both expanded and merged with what had always been true: the very essence of "being." It was unlike anything I'd ever known, and no description could do justice to the experience. In that instant, I was clearly and absolutely conscious of who and what I am. (3)

If the ego represents one part consciousness, one part latent unconscious and the other part not conscious at all, who then is observing the ego or self-consciousness and from where is that observation taking place? The observation is taking place from outside of the scientifically defined ego consciousness or neurobiological constructs. The observation comes from the soul which has its own consciousness and is joined beyond the veil of egoic consciousness to the Cosmic Consciousness via the spirit as Metaphysics teaches.

My focus was not intended to empirically define the ego or the veil but to posit that they are one and the same and that ego, consciousness and the veil are a complex component of our physical and ethereal existence. The importance of acknowledging that human beings are more complex than the applied sciences define through Biology, the varied and specialized fields of Neurobiology, Psychology, Sociology, Anthropology, Physics, Philosophy, Physics or even Metaphysics may have to be taken on faith. Even Dr. Jung concedes in his work that belief, whether true or not is valid. A direct quote from his essay, "The Undiscovered Self," Dr. Jung admits that: "We are entirely free to choose our standpoint; it will in any case be an arbitrary decision. There is, however, a strong empirical reason why we should hold beliefs that we know can never be proved. It is that they are known to be useful" (Princeton University Press, 127).

We need a divinely inspired multi-disciplinary understanding of the ego, the veil and the consciousness that is both within it and lies beyond it in order to truly help human lives to thrive in more open-minded and increasingly more effective ways. If we subscribed only to the biological aspect of consciousness, we would be missing the psychological potentialities of consciousness. If we subscribed only to the psychological aspect of consciousness, we would be missing the spiritual (not necessarily religious) or metaphysical aspect of consciousness or unity consciousness that could provide a greater sense of wholeness, health, and wellbeing.

The Ego is the Veil

Through my literature review and research, another picture begins to form for me that I believe underscores the need for greater understanding of the ego as the veil. An emerging view as I contemplate what I have researched is that the ego is that aspect of our souls that coalesces into physical matter and existence here in this three dimensional physical world. This view is somewhat similar to that expressed by Dr. Freud, however, I believe it goes further. I do not hold that ego equates only to consciousness for my own personal experience has taught me that ego equates to consciousness in the physical but I come to this conclusion from my own biased view following a near death experience. I experienced consciousness outside of my body while my physical body was deemed unconscious. The aspect of my personality described in psychological terms as ego was no longer part of my conscious experience. I was unconscious in the physical world but completely conscious in another unknown space or dimension perhaps, after my heart stopped beating.

I hold the knowledge from my personal experience that to truly understand an individual, we must reach farther than the limits of what is tested as truth with bias in merely the scientific or physical world and address individuals not as limited ego consciousness but as soul and beyond that, spiritual consciousness ever connected to the entirety of the collective that is, other aspects of consciousness existing here within this reality and possibly others.

These thoughts I hold cannot be proven in their entirety yet. The ideas remain in the realm of "mystery" at this point until with more time and study, we can determine more readily what is definitive versus provisional truth. Even still, I remain open to the possibility that my concepts and ideas fall to the realm of potentially yes, possibly no or ultimately maybe. That does not deter me in my approach to Metaphysical counseling or seeking to better understand all aspects of consciousness that defines us as beings. In fact, it forces me to keep my mind open and aware to potentialities as they emerge in our ever expanding field of awareness and ever growing understanding in the area of consciousness and its implications.

Chapter 9 – Considerations

From my exploration into the topic of consciousness, the ego as the veil, I begin to come to the conclusion that the life we experience here on Earth is the result of a conscious individuation from the Cosmic Mind or One Mind in the form of ego for the purpose of a physical experience in an individuated focal point of existence in a specific time. The ego is the veil that separates humanity from the Cosmic Mind or that, to us, which is unconscious or simply, not yet known. The veil does not separate us from our Source or sever the connection to that Cosmic Mind but rather obscures it through the existence of the ego. We remain part of the entirety of the cosmos, our cells, molecules and particles gathered as a density intentionally collected in a point of focus here in this now as are all entities in existence within this frame or dimension.

The ego exists as learned scholars and wise spiritual teachers will in unison agree. Where they all may diverge is on the purpose of the ego and understanding its related consciousness. In my dissertation, I posit that it is because of the ego that we have individuated from the One Mind or Cosmic Consciousness and this intentionally formed the veil between the physical conscious world and the world of unconsciousness, ether or the ethereal realms of the spirit. It is through the process of choosing individual experience that seems to separate us from our Source at a purely physical or conscious level. We did so in order to experience creating and the receiving of the gift and the use of free will from whatever Source or Force in this universe that created us. As a unified whole, we still exist, I think, as everything in creation is interconnected as well as interdependent. Others are beginning to join this body of thought.

Another wonderful work I encountered that describes this thought in part a little more comes from Eva Herr in her work, *Consciousness*, within the Introduction section. The author describes a moment in her life in which she became aware of her consciousness. She describes going to sleep one night during a troubling time and awoke with a new sense of purpose in that she moved away from "the dogma of materialism, vanity and self-consumed ideations" (Rainbowbridge Books, xix) and moved to a more full understanding of consciousness. She describes it within this same section as "The God force—behind everything that exists" and that accompanying this thought or feeling was "a powerful but simplistic idea of agape—the love for one's fellow man as one loves oneself, because we are all one."

It is not enough to become enlightened to the mechanics of the fullness of our physical existence; the 'hows and the whys' in which we have come to exist. These things are just the vehicles designed to carry forth our points of focus for an individuated experience of the wholeness of the Source of All That Is in order to truly experience and understand the significance of it. Perception affects the perceiver and thus the perceiver learns through his or her own perceptions of individual experience. If there were no veil of egoic consciousness, we might know the ending of the movie before the movie is finished playing and thus remove our ability to learn in the now moments as they pass as we intended. The ego is not something to be destroyed but rather, better understood.

Various disciplines describe the Cosmic or Quantum Whole with different languages. Many see the similarities in the words and descriptions and yet others see only a single source language with which to define our place in this world. I like to use the analogy of a tree. There is a beautiful tree planted on a beautiful green hill. How would a psychiatrist define the tree and its existence? How would an artist or poet describe the tree and its existence? How would a carpenter or mechanic see a tree? How would a reverend see a tree? How would a mystic describe a tree? How would a scientist or physicist define a tree? What about a botanist? Each would view the same tree and describe it in accord with his or her selected discipline or experiential perspective focus. There is no other way each could define the tree. But then what would happen if the Truth were explained that each perceiver from within his or her discipline was the tree or an integral part, thereof?

Like a perfect circle, each discipline has a degree from which they work within the construct of the circle. What if the reality of our individuated experience is the circle and yet there are increasingly ever more concentric circles overlaid upon our dimension of reality? Would it be too much for a simple human being to take in all at once? Does the ego create a sufficient veil that allows us to take in the information we need in bite-sized chunks that are much more easily digested and that make it easier to live our lives in our current point of focus for the experience we most desired?

What if our body, the physical body that we seemingly exist within is the ego or the point at which the spirit and soul meet the physical world? What if that ego is the tiny tip of the gigantic iceberg in terms of the divine aspects of the souls that we are and further yet, the spirit that lies beyond the veil? Beyond the spirit is the Source of All That Is and that is simply beyond a tiny particle's ability to comprehend. A tiny bug cannot comprehend the entirety of the universe cohesively and completely, as it hasn't got the capacity.

We have the potential for the capacity but our purpose and point of focus does not necessarily include understanding the entirety of the whole of existence precisely while our point of focus and materialization exists in the third dimension physically.

Understanding that we are not the limited, unimpressive mere egoic humans pursuing our desires to our detriment or betterment may yet buoy humanity as they work their way through the construct of this experience here in this world, in this dimension at this time. Physics theorizes and contemplates that our existence is not in a singular dimension but that it is quite possible that all that we see and experience has multiple layers of existence beyond that which we can readily comprehend.

The Ego is the Veil

Chapter 10 – Practical Application

Taking a bit of a break from the rigors of pure research and study, contemplating what I've come to learn, I've chosen a couple of select articles from my blog to share in this work as example of practical application of the concepts and how they may be applied in real-time, real life situations or interactions to raise awareness. I've replicated these articles in their entirety with only minor modifications. (See the Referenced Works section if you're interested in my blog).

Conscious Awareness

I am called by the name my biological parents gave me as well as the name under which I write but that is just a reference for my own personal point of focus here in the physical world. You can label me with other words if you wanted to but that wouldn't mean that you were accurate in your observation or perception of who or what you think I am. In fact, you can't know who or what I am in truth until you have that moment of crystalline clarity where you know who and understand what it is you truly are.

In your observations of those around you; you cannot see the totality of who and what they are. You may only perceive that which you are able or capable of understanding and you will project upon them as you most need to. You must realize that your perception is a result of simulations through the filter of your stored memories from which you have experienced this world. This means that with whatever or whomever you perceive stands before you, there will be a form of expectation in terms of what role you most need to cast someone into. If you look even now in your world you will find you are surrounded by the industrious, the loyal, the betrayers, the thieves, the wounded, the heroes, the angelic, the gifted and even the tortured, dishonest or even some you may term *villains*. But did you know that other people may not cast people in the same roles that you cast them in even if some others share your collective experience? Did you know or even care to realize that what you experience in another, at some level, you wish to experience or you would not experience it at all?

What does *all of this* mean? It does not hold the much overly simplified part of New Age "truth" in this concept that says what is in you is in others so if you see bad in others it is because you are bad or if you see only good in others, you are good. Think bigger, much bigger as this is a much bigger game you are playing in. What you are is consciousness, what you see is the expression of consciousness, what you experience is consciousness in the manner of your own perceiving. That consciousness you observe around you existing within their own points of focus here in 3-D Earth may be aware or unaware but it is or they are consciousness...or vibration if you will.

The entirety of the universe holds consciousness and our points of focus that represent our physical embodiment here in the land of three dimensional expression most commonly understood (at least in general) as *life on Earth* and our consciousness has been limited by those who forgot who and what they truly are so they had no means readily available with which to teach you the truth. You can choose to become aware or not as is your choice and I am here merely to paint a picture of another kind. And it is that picture that some will readily see and others will not. That thought does not change the truth of who and what you are. It also does not make real that which you perceive to be truth even if you "believe it."

You can ponder and contemplate the nature of the universe and it will be a wonderful endeavor but not near as wonderful as connecting to the center most integral part of the core of what you truly are. It would be wonderful if we could be so transparent that we changed the entire paradigm of our conscious awareness in this place in space-time perception. But until all are aware, this is not possible entirely. Consider the beauty and purity of what you truly are and as you consider this, know too the potential beauty and purity of all who stand before you exists regardless of roles you may have chosen to cast them in. Seek understanding and test your belief.

Belief IS only untested hypothesis that resulted from the simulations your own mind has run based on the data it has assumed as truth filtered through your memories of experience. So, test your hypotheses (are they real and can you say so with 100% objective certainty) and then you will begin to understand not only the truth about you but the truth of the other conscious points of focus in this realm. God bless each and every one of you as you make your journey of experience through this life. May you gain the awareness that you came here to gain. In love and in light, so it is.

Breaking the Veil of Illusion

Interesting it is how labels and accusations are so carelessly strewn about by some against others without understanding the truth. You see, your observations can only ever be filtered through your own biases, experience and other psychological filters. These observations form a perception of a thing or a person, and your perception, no matter how much you think is the definitive truth, is nothing but what you want to believe projected outward from within. This is done commonly and frequently with little understanding and in the absence of understanding these projections upon others come in the form of labels and names.

The labels created are not really representative of "the other" that is the object of your observation but is rather more descriptive of something much more familiar to you. Namely, what things lay hidden deep within you that you unknowingly project outward onto "the other?" The question those labeled often think in desperation is, "Why? Why would this person or that person label me in such a hurtful way?" Conversely, people can label you in what you think is a helpful way and still they are no closer to the truth of you. No person outside of you can truthfully determine your greatness or inadequacies properly without understanding the paradigm of The Whole. And I'll tell you, there are few who truly understand theparadigm of The Whole.

Imagine, if you will, the Internet of all things. There are those who study it as if it is an organism in and of itself. There are too many studies to specifically name but to review some of these concepts, simply conduct a Google

Internet search of "Study Internet Consciousness" and you'll come across numerous papers and studies on this topic. Now, back to my point.

It may be a confusing concept, but come along with me a moment as it might help you better understand one of the many metaphors of our existence here in this frame in the way we project ourselves (our consciousness). So, across the entirety of the globe (well in most places it seems these days), there are computer servers that are connected one to another through a vast physical network that creates the World Wide Web. The World Wide Web is a mass connectivity vehicle for our ability to "tune in" to others in the physical world. Now, each individual with a laptop, computer or smart phone taps into that source of collective information to connect and most definitely, individually project themselves into the whole of the World Wide Web. We are not the World Wide Web but the computers we use are a part of it by virtue of an Internet connection. Does that make sense at least at a high-level?

Okay, so stick with me another moment and I'll take you down a curve in the road to a much broader application of this concept which is not new at all but very old and understood by the Ancients, the Mystery Schools and even some great religious or spiritual teachers dating much further back than our history accurately documents. There is a Cosmic Consciousness, a single Source that was the impetus for creation. We each are like a tiny thought emanating outward from that Source but always and ever connected to that Source.

Through acknowledging connectivity with that Source we realize the connectivity we all hold similarly with each other. In this way, we are all one in that we are all the same thing in a way, thoughts projected from a Source. Now, this Source is infinitely powerful and creative and as you know from your own mind, your thoughts come from within you and once you create them, you send them "out there" and they become a thing unto themselves...energy, magnetic, emotion producing things we don't understand deeply enough. We are very much like those individual computers that plug into the World Wide Web. The thing is, we are never not connected to our Source and need nothing physical to connect to it other than understanding. As we connect to Source, we too are connected to each other.

Coming back to labels and observations now for a moment. If you observe with your thoughts another part of the connected Whole and ascribe labels to other parts of the Whole, in a way you are labeling yourself. What you perceive is not necessarily the truth of a thing or person and doesn't necessarily stand up to the rigors of empirical testing because your perception can

71

be skewed by assumption taken as fact or truth when there is not a single thing underpinning solidly the formation of your assumption or perception. But, because it seems to come from inside of your own head and maybe those thoughts generate some emotion or conviction behind it, it seems real enough and true enough. Given the limited set of facts within which most live and consciously operate, there is no reason to question the validity of your own assumptions, observations or perceptions. These processes are part of our instinctual nature. Truth, however, cannot be readily understood without valid facts and accurate understanding.

For ages people believed the world was flat and you could sail right off of the edge into oblivion. That was the common perception and agreement at a certain point in our history. That is, until some brave souls sought the truth beyond belief and sailed to the edge of the horizon and learned that the Earth was not limited in nature by being a flat two dimensional organism but in fact, it went on and on and around. These souls came back and shared their truth in the form of findings and then it became readily known that the world was, in fact, round. Then there was the idea that the sun and the planets revolved around the Earth. This was held as the only truth in the absence of facts. Even when the facts began to surface, they were outright rejected and labeled blasphemous likely due to fear caused by too many political or time-focused cultural factors I won't go into here but primarily a complete lack in understanding. But then, times progressed, scientific study progressed and new understanding dawned. We learned that the Earth revolves around the sun, and the sun is just the center of one universe and that there were more universes with suns spiraling through space by some impetus and force (Source, if you ask me). We then learned to go deeper within and study matter, energy and force and the things we took for granted or falsely held as belief was disproved by science. New windows and doors to the mind were flung open wide with new data and new horizons to consider, explore and discover.

Now, considering all of this, what if I were to tell you that what we perceive as real here, is still just an observation based on the limited or incomplete "facts" we hold as our beliefs about reality and what reality is? There is so much more than simply that which meets the eye. There is a world of consciousness we are not yet conscious of and the energy in the universe is connected and connected by the same Source that created all of it. That means we are all an integral and important part of the Source, a collective of existence with individualized points of focus in an agreed upon reality. The illusion of reality (life) as we perceive it is called Maya by the Hindus. (Check out the *Rigveda* for more understanding of the meaning of Maya).

Life as we know it is a grand illusion of sorts and to a great extent we are all delusional in our thoughts that what we see is real or that what we see, assume and perceive is representative of the definitive truth of a thing or a person. If you look back at all the explorations into the various aspects of life, existence and conscious understanding, you will see that the truth is not easy to discern by relying on our projected senses, our projected ideals, our projected morals and representations of belief we hold as truth. Our beliefs dissolve in the light of understanding. Why? We are growing and beginning to leave behind the time of small-minded thinking. Some of the Whole is aware of its delusion and thus seeks the freedom from it through understanding. Some of the Whole is unaware of its delusions and strive all the harder for the security of making their worlds more than real without understanding how that undermines their own limited perceptions of and about existence itself.

Coming full circle, realize that to perceive or label a thing does not define its truth. There is only one truth upon which we can rely and that truth cannot be defined by me for you. You must learn to understand the truth for yourselves. However, you will not find the truth of you in labeling your brothers and sisters who walk this Earth with you. In either positive or negative labeling, by raising others up higher than you or lowering them beneath you, you actually cage yourself in a prison of your own mind. The "All is Mind, the Universe is Mental" is a Hermetic principal from *The Kybalion*. This "physical life" is a construct of our making, collectively creating as we have been created. Sometimes trying to wrap your physical and limited mind around this concept makes you feel "mental" in a whole different way.

However, through patience, perseverance, allowing resonance, congruence, love, forgiveness, gratitude and an intent to understand, you can free your mind, body and soul from limited thoughts and embrace the whole of existence in a more liberating manner. The truth then is much better understood and the lesser acts of limited labeling or trapping yourselves in the veil of the ego would seem entirely insane.

Our assumptions and the need to label to begin with stem from natural biological processes in order for humanity to have a mechanism from which it can determine whether or not it is self and to preserve life and limb. Some of the data it takes in is filtered through memories of experience with emotions attached that aren't necessarily representative of definitive truth which can render it mere illusion.

Sometimes, the illusion of whatever it is the ego

wants only seems real but it isn't. The ego cannot tell the difference between a fact or an assumption without careful introspection and testing and so, will run its simulation processes resulting in the lining up of what it perceives to be the correct emotions with either. But, there is a deeper knowing part of your being whether you are in touch with it or not (your spirit) and it is the only thing that can guide you to the truth. The truth is more intuitively felt than understood with limited human words. We are by far above the limits of labeling even if we sometimes refuse to act like it. Attempting to become greater at the expense of another (which is a colossal illusion with quite fleeting benefits for the greedy or insecure ego) is meaningless and doesn't support you or secure your stature in a meaningful way that is everlasting.

If you tire of the victim-villain struggle for power, the only way to freedom is to understand you can't know what you don't know, so go and seek to understand the truth. Learn that what you give out to this world becomes you. Question the beliefs you assume or hold as truth. Offer this world forgiveness and love, offer this world peace and understanding and refuse to play into old programs that don't seem to get you anywhere. You end up chasing your tail for an ego feed that will never truly fulfill your deepest needs. Your deepest need is safety, satiety, understanding, to belong (and you belong to a very big Oneness in Source alone) and for love. You are love. Let that come to your mind first before acting on labels, before negative self or other judgments or to correct those negative self or other judgments that really don't serve you. Seek understanding and it will come and if you embrace it, you will be free.

Spaces Between

How many stories can one life hold? As I consider the stories that make up my own, I cannot help but wonder. There is still life in me to live in this realm and so it goes that there must be even more stories yet to come. I think some how perhaps, those to come shall be different than those that came before. Those that trail behind me like the wake on a river as a boat moves forward have shaped the reality of my presence in ways indescribable. It wasn't the events so much or even the people but the spaces in between. I come back to the sky again and see the similarities. Perhaps it is the darkness itself that holds up those stars where they hang so beautifully in the sky. *The space between...the space between*...my thoughts trail off and stop.

The space between may seem empty but it isn't, not by any stretch of the imagination. It seems that it is only those sleeping unaware of their slumber that do not realize the importance of the space between. The intangible knowings and etheric nature of the All of Everything knits together understanding and the seeing of themes as if one were connecting a constellation or two or three. All of life has meaning in terms of what it is you unconsciously wish to learn. I say unconsciously because there is an unconscious part of our very being directing and attracting those things the deepest core of us most wishes to learn. In that space between where feeling becomes thought and thought becomes charged with emotion to magnetic energy and then directed through perception, assumption...

The stories and events, the people involved are intrinsic aspects of our own nature and being and we just do not have the where-with-all to understand precisely how. It matters not at that level alone. What matters is learning to understand the clues to our own life purpose while standing in the truth of one's own light. But you'll not find that light reflected precisely in the gaze or interactions of others here in a three-dimensional Earthly focus. You must become aware of your own lack of awareness and begin to choose, begin to live consciously from the feeling parts of you beneath what we commonly consider consciousness to the true all-encompassing Cosmic Consciousness of existence. Then the entirety of the universe opens up and reflects right back into your own heart. Shutting down the perceptions and senses of the physical world doesn't close you off but opens you up to the unknown changing belief into the truth through experience turned to knowledge.

So, how many stories can one life hold? I'd say surely there must be as many as there are stars in a clear summer night's sky. And for what purpose can they truly hold but to teach us the meaning of life in the form of the less tangible lessons learned. It isn't just the things we see but the things we haven't yet learned to fathom. The truth isn't out there or just in here but some place in between.

The Ego is the Veil

Chapter 11 – Consciousness A New Frontier

Clearly, we have a need for greater understanding of consciousness and its additional stratifications. I believe that there is more to consciousness than just the Conscious, Preconscious and Unconsciousness as the field of psychology has defined them. Consciousness as a whole begins to look to me like dimensions might look to a theoretical physicist. It took us time to understand one-dimensional existence, two-dimensional existence, three-dimensional existence and the possibility that increasingly more dimensions exist. I don't see that any differently than the concept we simply term "consciousness." There are many people walking this Earth right now conscious but who seem wholly unaware that anything exists outside of themselves. There are those conscious who seem painfully aware of the various levels of awareness within consciousness and the complete lack thereof.

Through understanding consciousness, we can

begin to understand our existence and the Quantum Whole of which we are an intrinsic part. Without further study, we just keep flipping from one news channel to the next with varying levels of savory and unsavory news of happenings that seem obviously to me to stem from various levels of conscious awareness among humans engaging in the process of living their lives. Humans are as complex as the universe in some ways when you start to contemplate consciousness, energy, matter, vibration and existence as a whole. Everything matters and everything is relative but what is the common theme? I think it is consciousness for lack of better words and I think now, it is time to turn my focus to the next phase of my exploration into consciousness.

Consciousness is only a partially discovered and certainly only partially understood frontier that has the potential to neatly knit everything we see, feel and experience together. With further exploration of this frontier, I think we may find some very exciting things about our existence here in this frame. I think also that the study of consciousness cannot be contained as valid from the perspective of only one or a handful of the various applied science and other disciplines. As mentioned before, each discipline can only define consciousness from within the confines and constructs of their academic perspectives.

It will take some fearless pioneers unafraid to breakdown the walls, barriers, biases and prejudices working hand in hand to help us better understand the nature of what it truly is. I am not satisfied by the biological constructs alone. I am unsatisfied with the neurobiological constructs alone. I am unsatisfied with the philosophical and psychological constructs alone and I am still as yet unsatisfied with the theological and metaphysical constructs alone. I think if we work together we can find the common themes to all the various disciplines, come together, share notes, establish and test new hypothesis and attempt to draw new conclusions about what it truly is.

One thing I've been so excited to come across is Michio Kaku's new book, *The Future of the Mind*. In this book, Michio reviews the perspectives of consciousness from multiple disciplines. This famous theoretical physicist has a great mind for understanding and has thrown the physics view of consciousness into the ring and I couldn't be more pleased to see this. In Eva Herr's work, *Consciousness*, she solicits the view of consciousness by various learned scholars from multiple disciplines as well. Running across her work made me even more excited. "Yes," I thought! It is about time we stop the limited views and start charging into the view of many and see what understanding we can come up with by going beyond preconceived notions from times of old.

I have some ideas of my own and I intend to develop them further. They can be taken as food for thought or rubbish all-together I suppose. But that won't stop me and I hope it won't stop others from detaching from their limited scope of understanding and engage more fully in exploring this very exciting not entirely understood or fully explored frontier. The way I see it, such studies lead us to so much more. If the ego is intangible consciousness (maybe energy consciousness) meeting the third-dimensional world, what is behind that? Where does that something stem from and how can this understanding help us improve our lives or humanity as a whole? I believe this understanding is important. The ego is the veil that separates us from the Source; our Source.

Referenced Works

Capra, Frijof. *The Tao of Physics, 35th Anniversary Edition,* Massachusetts: Shambala Publications, 2010. Print.

"Dictionary.com." http://www.dictionary.com. Web.

Freud, Sigmund. *The Ego and the Id,* United States of America: Stellar Classics, 2013. Print.

Gomes, Michael. *The Secret Doctrine: Abridged and Annotated*, New York: Penguin, 2009. Print.

Harter, J.L. "Dream in Time." Http://www.dreamintime.com. Web.

Harter, J.L "The Ego is the Veil," unpublished doctoral dissertation, University of Sedona, 2014.

Herr, Eva. *Consciousness,* Virginia: Rainbow Ridge Books, 2012. Print

Hicks, John. "Consciousness: Still a Mystery." Institute for Noetic Science. 2007, Web. 2 June 2014

Hockenbury & Hockenbury. *Discovering Psychology: Sixth Edition,* New York: Worth Publishers, 2014, Print.

Jung, Carl G. *The Undiscovered Self,* New York: Signet, 2006. Print.

Jung, Carl G. *The Undiscovered Self with Symbolism and the Interpretation of Dreams,* New Jersey: Princeton University Press, 1990. Print.

Kaku, Michio. *The Future of the Mind,* New York: Doubleday, 2014. Print

"Merriam-Webster's Online Dictionary." Http://www.Merriam-webster.com. Web.

Ralston, Peter. *The Book of Not Knowing,* California: North Atlantic Books, 2010. Print

Roberts, Jane. *A Seth Reader,* California: Vernal Equinox Press, 1993. Print.

Rumi. *"The Ego is the veil between humans and god,"* Hindi Anmol Vachan.In (n.d.) Web. 2 June 2014

Schucman and Thetford. *A Course in miracles: Second Edition,* California: Foundation for Inner Peace, 1992. Print.

Tolle, Eckhart. *The Power of Now*, California: New World Library, 1999. Print.

The Ego is the Veil

Glossary of Terms

Applied Science: As defined by Dictionary.com means the discipline dealing with the art or science of applying scientific knowledge to practical problems; "he had trouble deciding which branch of engineering to study."

Assumption: the act of considering that a set of facts are true. The mind must make assumptions about the data it takes in from its environment in order to determine if what it faces is safe or unsafe.

Belief: Anything we believe is true even in the absence of the substance of that belief being proven true by Applied Science or Scientific Study.

Bias: When we apply a belief in our actions or perceptions of a person, place or thing. We form biases as a natural part of our instinctual existence just as we form our beliefs. Our biases may also represent definitive truths we have come to know. We may be biased in our approach to considering or taking in facts or evaluating data.

Biology: In summary, the study of the body and bodily functions.

Consciousness: I'm not quite sure we're able to accurately do this yet. Let us borrow from psychology for a moment and consider consciousness the Quantum Whole of our personal existence and that existence contains many striations or levels of awareness and potentially focus. A human is considered to be Conscious. For fun, let's try dictionary.com again and see what they say:

1. the state of being <u>conscious</u>; awareness of one's own existence, sensations, thoughts, surroundings, etc.
2. the thoughts and feelings, collectively, of an individual or of an aggregate of people: the moral consciousness of a nation.
3. full activity of the mind and senses, as in waking life: to regain consciousness after fainting.
4. awareness of something for what it is; internal knowledge: consciousness of wrongdoing.
5. concern, interest, or acute awareness: class consciousness.

Cosmology: Merriam-Webster.com defines Cosmology as:

1. *a* : a branch of metaphysics that deals with the nature of the universe
1.b : a theory or doctrine describing the natural order of the universe

2: a branch of astronomy that deals with the origin, structure, and space-time relationships of the universe; *also* : a theory dealing with these matters

Data: Individual pieces of information that exists in our perception.

Definitive Truth: That which can be objectively proven by scientific or other study that produces the result that supports the hypothesis put forth.

Ego: Sigmund Freud, in his works, defines the ego as the point where consciousness meets the physical world.

Facts: Details and information gathered and presumed to represent the truth of a person, place or thing.

Id: The instinctual part of our consciousness that is part of the ego consciousness as defined by Sigmund Freud.

Illusion: That which is perceived to be something which in reality is not.

Instinct: Simply put, Instinct represents our most basic and natural tendencies which are automatic.

Memory: Information stored within the brain based on experience of something or someone.

Metaphysics: Merriam-Webster.com defines Metaphysics as: *a (1)* : a division of philosophy that is concerned with the fundamental nature of reality and being and that includes ontology, cosmology, and often epistemology*(2)*: ontology 2 *b* : abstract philosophical studies : a study of what is outside objective experience

Neuroscience: Merriam-Webster.com defines Neuroscience as a branch (as neurophysiology) of the life sciences that deals with the anatomy, physiology, biochemistry, or molecular biology of nerves and nervous tissue and especially with their relation to behavior and learning.

New Age: Dictionary.com defines New Age first as an adjective as follows:

1. of or pertaining to a movement espousing a broad range of philosophies and practices traditionally viewed as occult, metaphysical, or paranormal.
2. of or pertaining to an unintrusive style of music using both acoustic and electronic instruments and drawing on classical music, jazz, and rock.

And then as a noun as follows:

3. the New Age movement.

Perception: The way that we take in and process information that we derive from our sense mechanisms.

Philosophy: Dictionary.com defines Philosophy as follows:

1. the rational investigation of the truths and principles of being, knowledge, or conduct.
2. any of the three branches, namely natural philosophy, moral philosophy, and metaphysical philosophy, that are accepted as composing this study.
3. a particular system of thought based on such study or investigation: the philosophy of Spinoza.
4. the critical study of the basic principles and concepts of a particular branch of knowledge, especially with a view to improving or reconstituting them: the philosophy of science.
5. a system of principles for guidance in practical affairs.

Physics: Dictionary.com defines Physics as the science that deals with matter, energy, motion, and force.

Provisional Truth: See Belief.

Psychology: In summary, study of the mind and its processes and actions.

Soul: From a metaphysical perspective, the soul is that aspect of our consciousness that inhabits the body, is a part of consciousness and can hold not only our memories but all memories.

Source: As used here in refers to Cosmic Consciousness, the concept of the All of Everything or God.

Spirit: As used herein, references that part of consciousness that contains the soul, ego-personality but is not limited to those things. The spirit is that aspect of our consciousness that most closely stems from the Source.

Spirituality: Refers to a state of perceiving, acting or functioning related to the concept of being part of something bigger than one's self.

Studies: Used typically in the applied sciences and other aspects of academia to gather facts and information related to hypothesis in order to determine if there are any results that may be statistically sound and significant in order to render a hypothesis as Definitive Truth or potentially plausible.

Synaptic Processes: Refers to activity within the brain involved in our bodily functions such as that involved in the autonomic nervous system, sympathetic nervous system or parasympathic nervous system, for example.

Theosophy: Dictionary.com defines this as:
1. any of various forms of philosophical or religious thought based on a mystical insight into the divine nature.
2. (often initial capital letters) the system of belief and practice of the Theosophical Society.

Madame H.P. Blavatsky was one of the Theosophical Society's founders back in the 1800s.

Truth: Is what is true and demonstrated as fact. Truth, unlike belief stands on its own apart from perception, perspective and assumption. Data is often gathered to determine the truth of a thing or statement. *Truth is True*, as a dear friend of mine has so often said. I like that definition the best.

Veil: Aside from Rumi's quote that put it quite aptly, the Veil is a concept as used herein to define that point at which unconsciousness separates consciousness. We've seen this used in comments such as "He spoke from beyond the veil."

The Ego is the Veil

ABOUT THE AUTHOR:

Rev. J.L. Harter, Ph.D (Jaie Hart) combines her spiritual vision and psychic insights with the world through her successful book series, popular blog and her websites. As an author of international repute, she has published over twelve books, including *Changing Perspectives – The Journey is the Destination, Expanding Horizons* and Life - *The Journey Continues.* In addition, she has also published her 'Reflections' series of poetry books. Rev. Harter's worldview combines the profoundly philosophical with everyday psychological aspects of the human condition. As a Mother, Intuitive, Reverend, Doctor of Philosophy and Reiki Master, she informs her works with a profound wisdom that never preaches, but rather takes her readers and clients through the troubles of the day with a deft assuredness that reinforces all that is positive. One central aspect of her work is her belief in reinforcing "Life Lessons" as a way to improve one's situation. For Rev. Harter, life's lessons must be learned to avoid having to repeat them, and it is this central theme which underpins her work. The intent behind her work is assisting people to see what is meaningful and possible throughout the world, and she operates as a spiritual catalyst for those who wish to shift their perspective.

Rev. Harter is currently working on a study of "Life Lessons" and a further exploration into consciousness and looks forward to further writing and teaching to assist people in the future.

Rev. Harter lives with her family in Southern, California.

www.ingramcontent.com/pod-product-compliance
Lightning Source LLC
LaVergne TN
LVHW091159080426
835509LV00006B/752